BEHIND CLOSED DOORS

The Reality Of Domestic Abuse

Devansh Roongta & Andrew Chen

Co-Authors: Vaibhav, Kenneth, Sahana, Vikranth

ISBN: 9798334671928

CONTENTS

Introduction

Overview

On average, nearly 20 people every minute are physically abused by an intimate partner in the United States. In one year, this equates to more than 10 million women and men alone (NCADV). Domestic abuse, home invasions, and other silent emergencies are some of the most severe and extremely traumatic crises that individuals can experience. Domestic abuse may involve a pattern of behavior in any relationship that is used to maintain power over an intimate partner and could range from physical and emotional to psychological, sexual abuse, or financial abuse. Moreover, it could also include threats that seriously affect personal safety, such as home invasions, which represent unlawful entry into a residence with intent to commit a crime. Other silent emergencies include situations of kidnappings, stalking, or forcefully holding a victim from communicating for help.

Cases of silent emergencies are very rampant. According to the World Health Organization, about one in three women worldwide has experienced physical or sexual intimate partner violence or non-partner sexual violence in their lifetime. According to the National

Coalition Against Domestic Violence, every minute in the United States alone nearly 20 people are physically abused by an intimate partner, amounting to well over 10 million women and men per year. Home invasions happen less frequently; nevertheless, as reported by the U.S. Department of Justice, there are about 1.03 million annually. Furthermore, in the United States in 2018, expressed by the National Crime Victimization Survey, approximately 3.3 million households encountered at least one type of property victimization.

These kinds of incidents have both long-term consequences on the individual and society as a whole. Domestic abuse victims indicated long-term psychological effects such as depression, anxiety, PTSD, and suicidal thoughts. The CDC reports that the annual cost of IPV exceeds $8.3 billion, combining medical care, mental health services, and lost productivity. Invasions into the home, similar to other silent emergencies, don't result in immediate physical harm only but are permanent traumas, like a general feeling of insecurity. The cost to society is enormous, ranging from health care and legal burdens to the long-term economic drain on communities.

Having these grim statistics in mind, technology has stepped forward to become the modern force of safety and power. It is due to new technologies that now provide exciting ways to help prevent, respond to, and recover from silent emergencies.

Tech Solutions

Modern technology offers new, innovative solutions that can be utilized in prevention, response, and recovery processes in case of silent emergencies. Of those technological developments, however, the most important ones are the mobile apps created for the purposes of personal safety. Apps, like Silent Safety, are designed so that in a moment of emergency, users do not have to raise much noise to contact police services. They are mostly fitted with a number of features such as GPS tracking, automated alerts sent to trusted contacts, and silently dialable alarm systems. For example, Silent Safety is able to communicate with 911 operators by sending location and critical information without requiring the user to speak, thus providing a lifeline during silent emergencies.

Wearable technology is also vital when it comes to personal safety. Devices like smartwatches or inconspicuous panic buttons can send out emergency alerts—if that is needed to be done—with very simple, at times concealed, gestures. These wearables can track a person's location in real time; in turn, alerting the authorities or other previously chosen emergency contacts as necessary. Businesses like Safelet have been developing bracelets that—once activated—alert a network of pre-selected guardians with said user's GPS location.

Besides, artificial intelligence and machine learning developments are now being used to predict cases of domestic abuse and prevent them. AI tools could look at patterns in communication, financial transactions, and even social media activities for hints of abuse. For example, researchers develop algorithms that flag potentially abusive behavior in texts and emails so as to prompt early intervention. Thirdly, machine learning models do an analysis of offender profile history to determine probabilities of reoffending, and resource allocation is recommended. Social media and digital storytelling have become a strong means of raising awareness and building a sense of community among survivors. Campaigns such as #MeToo and #WhyIStayed brought worldwide attention to the issues of domestic abuse and silent emergencies, urging survivors to come out and speak up for support. These digital movements have been instrumental not only in de-stigmatizing the experience of abuse but also in propelling legislative and social change.

Of course, implementation of technology into silent emergency situations is not challenge-free. Privacy and security concerns hit a high, as the very tools designed to protect the user can be exploited by abusers. Accessibility, ease of approach to such technologies, and user-friendliness are equally important when this solution seeks to propagate out to people who might be less tech-savvy or even to those who have poor access to better gadgets. One of the major challenges is those related to funding and resource allocation since most organizations develop and try to maintain such vital tools with very meager budgets.

However, the potential that technology holds in altering the face of silent emergency intervention is still vast. If we continue with eliciting feedback from survivors and experts relentlessly and take a sensitive approach to design, we can come up with resilient solutions that have real benefits. Of course, new technologies such as AI, IoT, and blockchain will further add to safety and empowerment, making for an optimistic future for the tech intervention of silent emergencies.

Challenges and opportunities are therefore identified at the intersection of technology and silent emergency situations. As we move through this shifting landscape, it will become imperative that the needs and experiences of victims are prioritized by using technology to offer safety, support, and empowerment. On this, innovation and collaboration can help set a future where people are protected, empowered, and silent emergencies are effectively responded to.

Section 1:

Case Studies and Real-Life Stories

1.1: Survivor's Story and Case Study

"Ceaseless- A Story of Courage and Recovery."

"Trauma is a fact of life. It does not,
however, have to be a life sentence."

— Peter A. Levine

It was at the dead of night. My neck loosened, my eyes blurred, and everything became a buzz within a moment. The sirens slammed into my ears, and they numbed from such a loud noise. Adrenaline kept rushing through my body, and I stared towards the dark road while several paramedics tended to my wounds. I laid on the cotton material of the stretcher as the paramedics noticed the back wound, adjusting my position so they could treat me appropriately.

But they were just too late. If only I could have dialed 911 earlier.

I was safe. And according to many that is the most important, but living to have to remember the paralyzing terror of the barrier between you and the intruders collapsing is the pain I will endure for the rest of my life. The next day, I visited therapy.

Therapist: You definitely have been through a lot, and it really makes it confusing for now. I suggest as much time with your family, friends, and more to recuperate from this event. Anything else?

Me: Nothing much, but I am still worried about my safety, if someone can breach my house so easily, then nothing is safe. My head drooped in the same way, and my blood began to pump rapidly as I tightened my grip on the padded chair underneath me.

Therapist: Try moving in with a friend, a family member, or anyone. You will feel much safer.

I jumped out of my seat and walked out of the room towards my car. I neglected my wallet and the therapist called out to me to stop since I forgot it. The drive back was. Something.

I screeched at a red light as my eyes dulled, my body stiffened, and I laid back into my leather seat, searching for the comfort of anything. Just anything.

What should I do?

You're unsafe.
You're useless.
You're just another pawn.

Don't come back.
Don't think.
Never, come, BACK.

You just need to remember the pain.
It is just that simple.

In that moment my eyes flashed closed as the door suddenly was kicked to splinters again.

You just need to forget it.

At that moment, my body felt the back wound again.

You just need to forget it.

In that moment my feet felt the splinters stabbing at my feet.

You just need to forget it.

You just need to forget.

My eyes opened to the car horns behind me, and I was blinded by the sun.

Subconsciously I knew how to drive back home, but the ride back I continued

to remember,
to endure,
and to suffer.

I parked, stopped the ignition, and stepped into the musty, humid air, unlocking the door of the condo. My head still continued to pound, and I was being punched with each heartbeat. It just seemed like the world had sprinted millions of miles ahead of me, and I was stuck at first plate enduring this pain.

I reached my room, slammed the door, and opened my computer, and by sheer chance, I found the motivation to open a document,

and began to type.

"I have always found a way to work during the summer, whether it be odd jobs in the local community garden or with a friendly neighbor. This was usually for me to generate a good amount of money for anything I wanted to do with friends or for myself. For this specific summer, I had found a job listing for watching over a house while the owner was gone for the week.

Seemed like something to fill my pockets quickly as well with a few hundred dollars and this also seemed to be an easy job. Best of all, no one else had applied yet. So I took the opportunity, reached out to the owner– Mr.Will– before stepping into my car for the long drive of around two hours.

The owner had listed tasks for the house, how to get in, and what I could or could not do over text in a rushed manner, so I spent the next few red lights dissecting what he had sent me.

"Take out the garbage. Vacuum the two living rooms and bedrooms. Mkae sure to CLEan the dining room. Fedethefish ASAP and find fodo in the basement, make surr to turn on fhte porchlight and lookthrough the computer. theres been alot of strange popups. let me know ASPA what thats about. Thanks again James." - Mr.Will. "PS- Keys under the bush in the back."

I laughed to myself that he had signed his name perfectly, but garbled his message in a rush.

Hours later, I finally saw his house in the clear distance. But I had to keep squinting to check if I wasn't hallucinating. It really was the largest mansion you only see from movies.

I've never seen or lived in any house close to this level. Everything screamed rich, his lush, well-cut grass, his sculpted bushes, and even the perfect brown door. It didn't even have a speck of age on it despite the house being around for several decades.

I pulled into the driveway and rushed to the back, prying open each of the perfectly-pruned bushes to search for the familiar shine of the keys. Soon enough, I saw them and scratched my arm pulling the keys out of the prickly branches of the bush. *That's fine.* I thought as I unlocked the door into the massive mansion.

Quickly I was greeted with a clean, distinct smell of cleaning products, as Mr.Will had set them on the ground next to the doormat. My socks slid almost perfectly around the glossy wood floor. My eyes burned from the glistening, reflective lights of the huge chandelier encompassing the mansion's first floor. *I love it.* And oh, I certainly loved this job. *Maybe he could go on vacation for perhaps a few more weeks.* I thought as I leaped into the pristine white bed of the guest room.

I settled into the mansion, and soon enough, began cleaning around and finishing the chores: Taking out the garbage, vacuuming both living rooms and bedrooms including the guest room I assumed, cleaning the dining room, feeding his extravagant fish, grabbing extra food from the basement, turning on the porchlight before night, and checking out his computer's issues.

Easy enough. I thought.

And sure enough, I was done within less than an hour, as I finished showering, I grabbed my summer homework. *Damn this is difficult.* Taking several APs next year wasn't helping with the fact that the symbols on my homework looked more like Latin than math.

The first part of the night was smooth, and I fell asleep almost immediately. But now that I am thinking about it, it is strange that there were so many people near the end of the street. I shrugged it off, but woke up extra early just to complete a few more problems with the homework.

Yet when I woke up the next morning at around 5:30,

it squealed open.

I suddenly tensed up, and began to walk as silently as possible, remembering to find a weapon for self defense as soon as possible.

Creeping into the kitchen I found a decently sharp knife that seemed good enough, and sprinted back up the stairs back to the guest room, locking the seemingly indestructible door and hiding under the bed, the splinters becoming unbearable as time had gone on. My phone was completely out of the question as the sound would be too loud. The only way out was to escape and dial them. Moving was not a choice. I had to stay silent to be safe.

"Getttt…thattt…piece…of…shitt!" One of them roared from the bottom floor. The entire house shook from the sheer power of the yell.

I heard dozens of heavy footsteps and yelling from the first floor, and they called to clear every single room on the second floor. The chandelier was shattered, and I heard almost everything downstairs be ransacked and destroyed. I clenched my knife close to my chest and closed my eyes but could not make a sound. *Hopefully I will be safe.* With no incoming saviors, I was truly on my own.

And so I waited.

Every moment was another hour.

My heart thumped so loud, I covered it to make sure they could hear nothing.

Each time something was destroyed into a million pieces at the entertainment of the intruders, I covered my ears to hope I would not become like those tables.

Every room was checked. Every single closet was opened and destroyed. Every sound consisted of screeching, slamming, and yelling from the intruders. They were drunk I assumed, from their complete disregard for their own cover by destroying the house. But then again, almost everyone was on vacation during this time of the summer.

BANG.

The doorknob squealed out in pain.

BANG.

The splinters of the door flashed everywhere, even under the bed.

BANG.

And the door was torn apart. The single barrier between me and the intruders was gone.

They laughed at the top of their lungs, even hurting my ears from the laughs turning into shrieks of entertainment, like they were watching the Roman gladiators battle.

My eyes blurred, my throat dried, and I pushed down the need to cough with my life. They threw around the desk, and slammed the laptop into millions of pieces. I peeked out just barely, and saw multiple of them carrying rifles and in casual wear. *Hopefully those aren't loaded.*

But before they left. I felt the entire room's presence on the bed. They looked at each other, one nodding, and the other taking a machete and stabbing it directly at the puffy blanket, mistaking it for a person sleeping in their absurd drunk state.

"You'rrree in deeeeep shhiit buddy if thattt killedd the kid man." One of the intruders joked. *What? How would they know I'm here? Why not Mr. Will?*

They lingered around, every moment I believed they would flip the bed over. But they screamed to flip the mattress and check every corner. Leaving an extra joking remark to find and kill me.

"Hreyyy honeyyy, I'mmmm homeee." The same intruder laughed at his own joke, leaving the others giggling beside them as they cut open the mattress and cut through the wood protecting me from them. The knife grazed my back, and multiple wooden splinters were inserted into my back as I clenched my fists, just hoping for the pain to go away.

PLEASE LET IT STOP.

GO AWAY.

STOP.

LET IT STOP.

My entire body clenched in pain from the wound on my back, but I knew the escape would be even worse. As they were in another room, I pushed past the pain. Trying to forget the pain, I remembered me and my parents, just enjoying another evening dinner at our local diner.

Dining on steak would be awesome.

Despite the unbearable pain, I slid my socks slowly down the stairs, descending each step with as much care as I could before one of the intruders heard me. As soon as one of them screamed to destroy the room, I made my move, fell on the floor multiple times, ignoring the splinters and broken glass all over my hands and feet.

I almost jumped out the backdoor as soon as I saw it creaking from the morning wind.

As soon as I stepped out, I breathed the morning smell of dew, heard the crickets chirping, and most importantly, feeling the pain reverberate throughout my body from my back.

Before I sprinted in my bloody socks all the way to the back of another neighbor's house, I hid behind a bush, waiting for them to start destroying another room to dial 911, loudly whispering into the phone, almost cringing from the amount of sound the both me and the phone made. I was glad they were drunk and preoccupied, or else they would have heard the ringtone coming from the phone.

I looked out of the bush, and spotted the best location for escape– the back of a neighbor's house, where I could chain houses, moving from each to each if necessary.

I believe I can do it.

I can do it.

I clenched my teeth, and pushed through the pain in my bloody back and both of my bloodied wood splinter and glass-filled socks, stood up, and made a run for it.

KEEP GOING.

DON'T STOP.

KEEP PUSHING.

DON'T GIVE UP.

I fell onto the wet grass once behind cover, embracing nature's scent while attempting to ease the pain as much as possible.

Within minutes, the emergency responders were called, and I crawled out from my hiding place, allowing them to spot me and carry me in a stretcher back to the ambulance.

Nothing was said. A few introductions. A few nods. A few extra breaths. But I stiffened, and let everything speak for itself. My neck loosened, my eyes blurred, and everything became a buzz within a moment.

And for the entire ride back, I had to

to remember,
to endure,
and to suffer.

Staying silent that night saved my life. But any opportunity to call the police sooner could have saved me earlier."

— James out.

Case Study of Ceaseless: A Story of Courage and Recovery

There have been multiple stories of incidents like the story of Ceaseless occurring, and it is mostly due to a lack of silent notification devices or apps that these need to occur. This can lead to unnecessary trauma, wounds, and hospital expenses later down the line, and is incredibly difficult to deal with. Having a technology solution similar to Silent Safety, or an app or button that you can silently notify the authorities with whenever a situation presents itself in which you must stay silent to be safe i.e. domestic abuse or home invasions, can lead to completely different outcomes.

In real life, there have been many cases of victims not being able to receive the appropriate treatment or help in situations as dire or dangerous as Ceaseless. A property crime happens every 4.4 seconds according to Forbes, and many are left in situations in which making noise will lead to their severe injury or death. It is truly a race against the clock for first responders to arrive, and most of the time, it leaves the person in severe physical or mental trauma, as they were left to fend for themselves.

Had our main character, James, had access to an app similar to Silent Safety, then he would have been able to alert the authorities much earlier and have been able to spare the unnecessary wounds or trauma dealt to him. Clearly, in the situation of him hiding under the bed, ensuring that help was on the way would have allowed him the flexibility to make many more choices i.e. escape directly when the intruders fled from hearing the police sirens.

Now, much of the reason why James was able to survive this traumatic encounter was due to his pure grit and endurance. Had he just sat down and given up from the pain of all the glass or wooden splinters all over his hands and feet, or stayed under the bed, almost nothing would have been done and his severe injury or death would have been guaranteed.

This type of grit through injury is a theme commonly found in close-call stories of home invasions which inspired this.

There were many crucial moments within the story where James was injured or had a chance to escape that he could have capitalized on had he had an app similar to Silent Safety. Seeing the situation first hand, James was immobilized in terms of his decisions, and this is the whole reason for writing a story like this. Being able to provide readers around the world with a story to simulate as if they were in a situation or feeling the trauma like James is a powerful tool that I attempted to capitalize on for Ceaseless. Within the story, it is clear that James had almost no options, any slight movements would lead to the discovery of his hiding place, calling 911 would be too loud, and escape was hindered by the presence of multiple strong intruders.

If you notice, I also had to mention how he grabbed summer jobs as soon as he finished university for the year, this is to emphasize just how little he had in savings to spare. This is the exact reason why something like Silent Safety would have helped him to save hospitalization costs effectively. Had he had law enforcement come earlier, he would have had less serious injuries– the only injury he had before he fell escaping was on his feet while hiding under the bed. Yet being forced to escape, he fell from the pain of the previous splinter from under the bed onto the shards of glass and wooden splinters all over the ground on the downstairs floor. My main message from this is that technology similar to Silent Safety can be incredibly useful in limiting hospitalization costs.

Now it is clear, within this fictional story, had James possessed a tool similar to Silent Safety in the immobilizing situation that he was in, he could have had less trauma from the event, limited his hospitalization costs, and cut down the amount of wounds he did have.

1.2: Community and Organization Initiatives

Technology Companies and Domestic Abuse

With so many issues, there is always a response to fight back, and this is exactly what thousands if not hundreds of thousands of companies, nonprofits, and advocates have pushed such safety to victims of various attacks, such as domestic abuse. There have been significant actions implemented between technology companies around the globe from the hard work of domestic abuse organizations stretching advocacy across every continent of the world!

Significant examples of technology companies creating new features just for domestic abuse or home invasions, where Norton and Techsoup have partnered with various nonprofits i.e. the Safe Shelter Collaborative to create features in their services like active but secret location monitoring and interception of online messages or emails.

Technology companies stepping it up and even creating a new product line with dedicated employees would be companies such as the SoSecure mobile app, where employees can remotely trigger an emergency alarm if anything happens to the victims, allowing law enforcement to show up as soon as possible. Some incredible features that SoSecure offers is adding a list of emergency contacts that are notified if the silent alarm is activated. They also are notified if the victim is not responsive for a few days on end. All of these features are meant to help domestic abuse victims as much as possible with as little suspicion from their attackers.

Incredibly, some organizations that do not prioritize technology as their mainstream revenue or mission have even taken up the mission to protect domestic abuse victims, such as Cornell's Clinic to End Tech Abuse (CETA), where they provide services to protect victims from stalking from their abusive partners. Another company is Uber, where they even offered 50,000 free rides to safety for domestic abuse victims with additional resources. A company that offers pro bono, or free legal services for domestic abuse victims is Palladin, which was created jointly with the American Bar Association. This allows domestic abuse victims to access legal services easier without having to stay dependent on their abusive partners for monetary support.

An incredible example of a technology company that has worked one on one with police departments is Silent Safety, this company has been able to create an accessible app for anyone in dire need of help but they must stay silent to be safe. The app consists of a button to press to automatically contact the authorities silently and multiple fields of information to fill so the police automatically can find you in order to assist.

There are thousands if not hundreds of thousands of advocacy organizations dedicated toward victims of domestic abuse and home invasions to support them. This mission is not finished yet, and they will continue to battle for the support of victims for all traumatic scenarios.

Section 2:

Understanding Domestic Abuse & Silent Situations

2.1: Types of Silent Emergency Situations

Domestic Abuse

Domestic abuse, often referred to as intimate partner violence, is one of the leading issues in society today, estimated to affect hundreds of millions globally. Further, abuse is defined as physical, emotional, psychological, sexual, and financial. While all types of abuses are different in nature, all have one common thread: one person holds power and control over the other. As defined by the World Health Organization, nearly one in three women worldwide have experienced intimate partner physical or sexual violence at some point in their lives. Just from this single fact, one can fathom the pure scope and size of domestic abuse as a silent emergency.

Abuse of a physical nature involves the use of physical force against the victim, which causes injury or pain. More common manifestations include hitting, slapping, punching, kicking, choking, and the use of weapons. In most cases, physical abuse is accompanied by continuous threats of further violence, which creates an atmosphere of fear and intimidation. Although some classic marks of injury may be seen, many injuries are concealed or passed off with a plausible explanation by the victim out of fear for the abuser. Such a cycle of physical abuse may often lead to serious health complications, such as chronic pain, gastrointestinal disorders, and neurological damage.

Emotional or psychological abuse is those actions that impair an individual's self-esteem and shatter emotional well-being—verbal assaults, threats, intimidation, humiliation, and manipulation. Unlike in the case of physical abuse, there are no visible marks of emotional abuse, yet it can have the same or even more jarring effects. Many victims turn to depression, anxiety, and other mental disorders. It is supported by the Centers for Disease Control and Prevention that in most cases, emotional abuse usually precedes physical violence. Emotional abuse thus leads to a situation where the self-esteem of the victim is at its lowest, feeling trapped and powerless to get out of the abusive situation. In the long term, the effect may be post-traumatic stress disorder, suicidal thoughts, and serious depression.

Sexual abuse in a domestic setting incorporates any sexual activity wherein the act is nonconsensual. It also includes undesired touching, forced intercourse, or coerced sexual activities. In most cases, sexual abuse is used as a means of control and domination that eventually leads to serious psychological trauma in victims. The NSVRC reports that sexual violence within intimate relationships is vastly underreported and, therefore, hidden but vitally important. Such can result in highly diversified physical and psychological effects among the victims of sexual abuse, including sexually transmitted infections, problems with reproductive health, and deep emotional trauma. Part of these consequences include stigma and shame, which may thwart outreach. Help-seeking by a victim is prevented or deterred in many instances due to the stigma and shame associated with sexual abuse, further isolating victims from support.

Abusers reduce the victim's potential to support themselves by limiting them to financial resources, and eventually, leaving the abusive situation. This can take the form of denying the victim access to money, forbidding her or him to work, or sabotaging employment opportunities. Many victims of abuse are held in the cycle of abuse by financial dependency on the abuser; without any other means, they cannot leave the relationship. The National Network to End Domestic Violence states that 99% of domestic violence cases involve financial abuse. It is the best strategy for bringing about devastating effects in terms of long-term instability and debt. Once a victim has finally managed to leave the abusive relationship, it can become difficult to rebuild financial independence.

In most of these cases, silence becomes a survival strategy for the victim. The fear of retaliation, shame, and the hope that the situation will get better often compel the victim to endure the abuse quietly. Technology can be a vital lifeline in such scenarios by giving discreet ways of obtaining help without alarming the abuser. For instance, mobile applications that offer a silent alert to authorities or trusted contacts are very useful in such scenarios. These tools allow victims to request help without any noise, therefore diminishing the risk of escalating the violence.

Home Invasions

Another nightmarish, silent emergency situation is home invasions, wherein the victim is hobbled in his or her ability to make noise or attract authorities: a crime where one gains unlawful entry into a dwelling while there are occupants present, with an intention to conduct another crime, like burglary, assault, robbery, or even kidnapping. Still, according to the U.S. Department of Justice, there are approximately 1.03 million incidents of home invasion each year, pointing out a strong element of risk to personal safety. Most home invasion burglars tend to be forcefully intrusive over the victims in the house. They threaten their victims with either death or violence; therefore, the victims must be silent to avoid antagonizing them further. Such an event's trauma does not just stop at the physicality of the harm caused. It can also mean long-term anxiety, PTSD, and insecurity. Long-term fear instills hypervigilance and a fear of ever feeling safe in their own homes after the invasion has taken place.

The methods employed by intruders during home invasions can vary widely, yet often they have elements of surprise and violence. Intruders can force their way in through windows or doors, threaten weapon-armed occupants, and bind their victims to prevent them from reporting to authorities for assistance. Other times, home invasions are premeditated where intruders eye certain homes as potential opportunities. This premeditation is what infuses the forces of fear, helplessness, and vulnerability on the victims of this crime since they feel they were picked on deliberately.

Technology has so advanced that it is a very helpful tool in reducing the risks associated with home invasions today. State-of-the-art security systems, with access to silent alarms and motion detectors, coupled with live surveillance, are able to alert authorities without alerting intruders. Smart home devices, including video doorbells and remotely accessed alarm systems, raise the level of safety by allowing occupants to respond and monitor dubious situations discreetly. It is possible that some devices will turn on an alert to the homeowner's phone, whereby he or she can raise an alarm to authorities even if not at home. Those are the capabilities of some security systems: two-way communication features, which let one talk to the intruders or emergency response without being physically present.

Even with advances in technology, the psychological effects of home invasion cannot be belittled. Indeed, many victims experience feelings of violation and insecurity as the place primarily considered safe and secure—the home—translates to fear and danger. Counseling and support services are thus an integral part of enabling victims to recuperate from the traumatic experience of a home invasion. They may provide emotional support, coping strategies, and practical advice on improving home security to avoid further occurrences.

Kidnapping and Abductions

Kidnapping and abduction are the most serious forms of silent emergency situations wherein the victim is taken forcibly and held against such a person's will. This may take place because of familial disputes, human trafficking, or simply some criminal act committed by any random person. According to the FBI, approximately 840,000 children have been reported missing in the United States annually, and in a large number of these cases, these children were kidnapped by non-family members. Whereas most of these cases are solved rather quickly, the fear and uncertainty among the victims and their families during the abduction is deep.

In a kidnapping situation, the victim's communications are severely inhibited. The victim may be physically tied, held in isolated areas, or kept under constant observation by the abductors. The fear of violent consequences if they ever try to escape or make noise is a very potent inhibitor. The flop of psychological trauma on kidnap victims is very deep and has a far-reaching consequence on their mental health and well-being at large. Victims often experience extreme stress, anxiety, and post-traumatic stress disorder, which can be persistent for years after they are physically free.

The situations in which people get kidnapped are quite different. Some are kidnapped for ransom, whereby the kidnappers demand money or other concessions in exchange for the victim's release. Other cases of kidnappings can be attributed to personal vendettas, human trafficking, or even ideologies. In all cases, the common factor is extreme control and isolation over the victim. This can make it very hard for a victim to even send out a cry for help since she is often completely cut off from any means of communication.

Technology has Contributed Greatly to Ending Kidnappings: Scores of kidnappings have been solved through the use of technology. In this modern age, tracking devices will be needed, most of them embedded in personal devices like watches and phones, to easily locate and rescue victims. There are, in addition, mobile apps designed for the silent sending of distress signals to previously chosen contacts or even the police. Such tools are very important in giving victims a discreet way to get help without alarming the captors. For instance, using the application "My SOS Family", you can silently trigger an SOS alert to your contacts, sharing your location.

Public awareness and public education, too, are very essential to the prevention of kidnappings. Such programs have been known to save lives by teaching children and adults about the dangers of abduction, the ways to identify potential threats and what to do in case one is taken. It is collaborative efforts by schools, community organizations, and law enforcement that provide such educational programs, always emphasizing vigilance and acting fast in preventing or responding to kidnappings.

The psychological effects of kidnappings are enormous and long-term. In most cases, victims need massive counseling and assistance in order to get back on their feet. Sessions with a therapist can enable the victim to work through the kidney's experience, build coping techniques, and regain a feeling of safety. Support groups can be valuable too; within the support groups, they will have an avenue to open up about their experiences and bond with people who have gone through similar experiences.

Other Situations Where Speaking
is Not the Best Option

Situations of silent emergencies include much more than domestic abuse, home invasion, and kidnapping. They are in fact outnumbered by the list of other situations where an individual needs to remain silent for safety. Stalking is also one such situation where the victim is being constantly monitored by the stalker. Making any noise or openly attempting to get help in such a situation aggravates the danger. According to the National Center for Victims of Crime, within one year in the United States, 7.5 million people report being stalked, most of whom report high levels of fear.

Stalkers have developed varieties of ways to control and threaten their victims, which include trailing after them, slashes by mail, or even break-ins into houses. There, too, technology can assist in making a victim feel trapped and helpless as a consequence of stalking's intrusive and relentless nature. Mobile apps that log and report incidents of stalking discreetly can aid a case against the stalker, all while keeping the victim safe. Moreover, GPS tracking devices and personal safety alarms lend peace of mind and additional safety in the situation.

Another context where silence might be required is workplace violence. Employees are under threats of violence from other staff or even customers. In this regard, the ability to raise a discrete alarm to security or authority becomes very important. Technology such as panic buttons, silent alarms, and discreet communication apps can facilitate calling for help without antagonizing the situation. According to OSHA, nearly 2 million American workers report being victims of workplace violence every year. Having the ability to quickly and quietly alert security can prevent situations like these from escalating and save employees from harm.

Public spaces can also be sites of silent emergencies. When there is an active shooter or just after an instance of a terrorist attack, the best strategy to adopt for survival is to be very silent and hidden. Mobile apps that provide real-time information and silent channels for contacting authorities in such situations can be lifesavers. For example, the "Run, Hide, Fight" application tells the user what to do in an active shooter situation, including how to communicate silently with law enforcement.

The role of technology in such silent emergency situations is irreplaceable. It offers innovative ways of silently reaching out for help, from mobile apps and wearable devices to sophisticated security systems. By realizing the large spectrum of situations that silent emergencies can encompass, we can really appreciate how important technological interventions are in giving safety and support to the concerned person.

2.2: Psychological and Emotional Impact

Trauma and Stress Response

Silent emergency situations, like domestic abuse, home invasions, and kidnappings, have a tremendous psychological and emotional impact, which is deep and long-term in its impact; trauma and stress responses are immediate and intense reactions to such extreme conditions. Upon the occurrence of a person experiencing such crises, his body and mind go into an increased awareness stage, often known as the "fight-or-flight" reaction. This is an evolutionarily developed response to provide a chance at survival from a life-threatening event. In the case of domestic abuse or other silent emergencies, this inability—due to the required silence—may increase mental trauma.

Continuous abuse or a sudden violent incident can trigger the release in the brain of such stress hormones as adrenaline and cortisol in an abused individual. These hormones prepare the organism either to fight the danger or to run away from it. The heartbeat rises, muscles contract, and senses sharpen. While these physiological changes are adaptive in the short term, their chronic activation due to stress can result in severe health problems. Chronic stress affects the cardiovascular system, weakens immune functioning, and can lead to digestive problems and chronic pain conditions.

In domestic abuse situations, many victims will have to endure this heightened stress response on numerous occasions, a situation termed complex trauma. Domestic abuse victims live in high arousal, on constant alert for the next thing that might happen—another bout of violence or manipulation. This will, in turn, lead to a number of psychological manifestations, including anxiety, depression, and PTSD.

PTSD is a possible result of having gone through or witnessed life-threatening events. It is characterized by recurrent intrusions of memories in the form of nightmares or with a high degree of anxiety, so as to affect normal daily living. In such situations, victims often report reliving the trauma in the form of a flashback, where they feel that they are going through the experience again. These intrusive thoughts can be triggered by apparently neutral stimuli that the brain has chosen to associate with such activities: perhaps some smell, sound, or place. Avoidance behaviors are also typically associated with PTSD; at all costs, there are efforts to avoid reminders of the trauma, and these reminders include people, places, and activities that the victim used to enjoy.

Trauma can also impact cognitive functions from a psychological perspective. People who have been continuously abused or have gone through some other catastrophic situations in their lives develop problems related to concentration, memory, and decision-making. Being constantly aware and putting the mind in focus for survival could alter the way a human brain handles and stores new information. This is a cognitive impairment that must manifest in different areas of life, be it employment, education, or even personal.

Another critical factor in the lives of silent emergency victims is sleep disorders. Sleep issues, such as insomnia, nightmares, and night terrors, are common in people who have undergone trauma. The hyperarousal that occurs in PTSD may cause difficulty initiating or maintaining sleep and may result in chronic fatigue, which will raise anxiety and depression. Poor quality of sleep impairs the performing matrices generally and may make it harder to get over the daily stressors.

Another protective mechanism is the emotional numbing that usually accompanies trauma. The victim of manifold atrocities detaches from one's feelings in order to ward off the pain brought about by such experiences. While emotionally numbing a situation may really help a person in taming their immediate emotional response, over long-term scenarios, it may lead to difficulties in experiencing and expressing emotions. This detachment can bring about problems relating to others and lower the quality of life in general since the victim is unable to have close relationships or engage in activities done earlier and appreciate them.

Trauma extends beyond the individual, affecting families, communities, and society in general. For instance, major cases of secondary trauma are affirmed in the families of the victims since they are experiencing the aftereffects of what occurred to their loved ones. The children are the worst affected by witnessing domestic abuse or experiencing the aftermath of home invasions and kidnappings. They might develop behavior problems, lag behind academically, and display some problems in forming healthy relationships.

Communities affected by high proportions of these quiet emergencies also have to put up with higher crime rates and depressed home values and claims on trauma present an enormous cost to society: claims on healthcare expenditure, lost work performance, and burdens on the legal and social support systems.

Long-Term Effects on the Victims

The overwhelming and far-reaching long-term effect of trauma caused by silent emergency situations can affect all spheres of a victim's life. One such severe long-term consequence is that the development of chronic mental health disorders can ensue. Anxiety and depression are usual in survivors of domestic abuse, home invasions, or kidnappings. Such conditions may persist for years after the danger has passed and usually require long-term therapeutic interventions.

Trauma survivors are often prone to various anxiety disorders, including general anxiety disorder, panic disorder, and social anxiety disorder. These may further manifest into excessive or continuous worrying, recurring attacks of panic, or unreasonable, excessive fear of social situations. Among the major symptoms of anxiety are constant states of fear and vigilance, which impose limitations and handicaps on day-to-day activities and result in individuals' isolation from their support systems.

Another very common long-term effect of trauma is depression, characterized by feelings of extreme sadness, hopelessness, and a lack of interest in previously enjoyable activities. Survivors often bear feelings of worthlessness and guilt, even to the point of self-blame for the abuse or violence they may have endured. This kind of self-blame could be very strongly implanted in the victim by the manipulative actions of the abuser, further indenturing her into negative self-description.

Long-term trauma victims can also succumb to complex post-traumatic stress disorder. C-PTSD has almost the same features as PTSD except that it adds specific symptoms such as problems with emotional regulation, consciousness, self-perception, and interpersonal relationships. The victim may feel estranged from themselves or others, be sad most of the time with suicidal thoughts, and often find it hard to stay in intimate relationships.

Substance abuse is also one of the long-term effects of trauma. Many survivors resort to alcohol or drugs as a form of survival tactic to help them get through the unbearably painful and stressful experiences of what has happened to them. Substance abuse may alleviate emotional distress temporarily, thus aggravating the problems of addiction. This complicates the recovery process even more for the victim.

This is also the case with regard to problems in physical health. Chronic stress can lead to a host of physical disorders, which include cardiovascular disease, diabetes, disorders in the gastrointestinal system, and autoimmune diseases. If stress persists for a long time, then the constant barrage of stress hormones weakens the immune system, and such people become more susceptible to infections and diseases.

Trauma can go deep into the roots of interpersonal relationships. Survivors of domestic abuse, home invasions, and kidnappings are known to live with distrust and are often socially isolated. One main characteristic is troubled intimacy due to the fear of being vulnerable again and getting hurt. This strained or non-existent relationship can further isolate the victim from much-needed social support.

Another long-term effect of trauma is economic instability. Most survivors face financial problems resulting from financial abuse, loss of employment, or medical and psychological expenses for treatment purposes. The impact of economic insecurity can render the victim poor and dependent, which complicates the process of rebuilding life.

The consequences in children, particularly those who witness or go through major traumas, are even more disastrous. Brain development is hampered during childhood trauma. Developmental problems may be reflected within the child's cognitive, emotional, and behavioral functions. Thus, the traumatized child can experience educational failure, become either disruptive or withdrawn and not be able to develop healthy attachments and relationships. The effects of childhood trauma stretch into adulthood and affect every aspect of a person's life.

Though phenomenally deep and far-reaching, trauma does not have to be the last word in one's life. A myriad of support services—psychotherapeutic intervention, medical care, and social support—are offered to the survivor to help their lives get back on their feet. Indeed, CBT has been very effective for the different conditions caused by trauma, particularly in causing PTSD. This therefore enables the establishment of thoughts that are distressing and how to change them, hence survival with healthier coping mechanisms.

The support groups very often turn out to be equally important in the recovery process by providing a sense of belonging and understanding. Reaching out to others, especially those who have gone or are going through similar situations, does much to reduce feelings of isolation and offers real advice and encouragement.

Technology has also developed new tools for trauma survivors over the past few years. Locations with mobile apps created for mental health can make access to therapy and support discreetly done, hence removing a sense of stigma or exposure when one seeks help. Another area is virtual reality therapy, where people can be brought into an immersive environment in which they can deal with their trauma.

Ultimately, recovery is individual. It requires medical, psychological, and social support, along with time and patience. Unless there is an understanding of the deep impact of trauma and how inclusive the support has to be in most walks of life for the survivors, care during situations of silent emergency cannot be administered effectively.

2.3: Barriers To Seeking Help

Social Stigma and Shame

One of the major barriers to seeking help during such silent emergency situations, including cases of domestic abuse, home invasions, and kidnappings, is the social stigma and shame associated with their happening within personal experience. Victims are left with feelings of deep shame and guilt as if they are to be judged by others if they ever tell anyone about their situation. This stigma is very hard to deal with in situations involving domestic abuse, where cultural values and norms might put pressure on somebody to hold on to family harmony or adhere to traditional gender roles.

In most societies, victims of domestic abuse are often blamed for their situations. They can then be asked why they stayed in the relationship or why they did not fight back against the victory-line sort of thinking. The fear alone of not being believed or even of being judged will hinder a victim from reporting the issue to friends, family members, and authorities. This isolation deepens as the emotional and psychic effects of abuse get more intense, binding victims into the trap of silence and suffering.

There is also much stigma attached to home invasions and kidnappings. In these cases, victims often feel that they could have prevented the incident or should have been better able to protect themselves and their families. The perceived inability to do so further stigmatizes the failure to protect one's self and family, engendering feelings of inadequacy and self-blame, and therefore further acts as a deterrent to seeking the help and support required. Moreover, such incidents are responded to by the media, which sensationalize the crime rather than emphasize that the believer needs support and recuperation. Sensationalism adds to the stigma and dissuades victims from coming out into the open.

For instance, a woman who is being tortured by domestic abuse might well be afraid that if she were to tell someone about the problem, she would be seen as weak or somehow to blame for the abuse. She may also be afraid of being shunned by her community or by the judgment of friends and family. Such stigma is thus a powerful element of dissuasion, keeping her from coming out to seek the help she desperately needs. Likewise, a victim of a home invasion could feel too ashamed about the failure to protect one's home and loved ones and so be uneasy about reporting to the authorities or even seeking counseling.

Stigma often extends to the professionals and institutions that are supposed to help in a silent emergency situation. Healthcare providers, law enforcement officers, and social workers may carry some bias or misconception against domestic abuse victims, home invasion victims, or kidnapping victims due to which their responses may be less than adequate and sensitive. Victims encountering such people may feel further marginalized and/or alienated from seeking help in the future.

Fear of Retaliation

Another critical barrier to help-seeking is fear of the abuser's or perpetrator's retaliation. The threat of further violence in situations of domestic abuse becomes a very strong deterrent. Abusers often use intimidation tactics to instill fear in their victims by warning them of severe consequences if they attempt to leave or seek help. Such fear is not without a rational basis, as many victims who do try to escape or report the abuse face escalated violence.

The fear of retaliation, equally paralyzing for many victims of home invasions and kidnappings, is another type of barrier. Sometimes offenders threaten to hurt their victims or their relatives if they contact authorities or go to a hospital. This threat only compounds the original event's traumatization, which keeps these victims on high alert, always looking over their shoulders. In this cycle of fear and helplessness, victims find it impossible to talk of any kind about help in the face of a perceived or actual risk of further harm.

In many cases of domestic abuse, abusers will make explicit threats of violence in order to keep the victim from speaking out. Such threats may be physical—promises to harm or kill—and/or perhaps even more subtle—in the form of threatening to take children away or report one to immigration authorities. It drains a victim so much psychologically that he/she cannot even begin to contemplate seeking help under constant threats.

Further, abusers usually understand or know a lot about their victim's fears and vulnerabilities. They will manipulate the victim to maintain an upper hand, making them believe that trying to get out of the situation is likely to lead to worse consequences. An example may be that a victim does not dare to seek help out of fear that the abuser will harm their children or any other close relatives as a consequence of their actions, thus the risk becomes too great to do anything.

Financial Dependence

One giant hurdle is financial dependence, especially in the case of domestic abuse. Usually, the abuser will like to limit the access of the victim to financial resources, and in turn, it will not be easy for them to leave the relationship or get other living arrangements. Because of economic abuse, individuals may withhold money, control access to bank accounts, prevent the victim from working, or seek to undermine employment opportunities.

Where there is no financial independence, therefore, the victim may feel entrapped, unable to afford the associated costs of leaving the abuser. Lack of finances also limits access to legal representation and medical care. This entrenches the victim further in their condition. In fact, financial dependency is a powerfully effective controlling instrument, and how to overcome it all depends on external agencies or support networks for help and resources.

For example, an economically dependent woman may not have the means to pay for rent, food, and transportation if she leaves her abusive partner. In this way, such financial insecurity can render leaving an impossible step to take, especially when there are children involved. The fear of homelessness and poverty can thus hold victims in situations of abuse much longer than might otherwise have been the case.

Moreover, the legal and logistical challenges that must be surmounted to achieve a state of financial independence are too overwhelming. For instance, a victim is required to navigate through bureaucratic systems when applying for public assistance or affordable housing and to find employment. In the event that there is no substantial support system for the victims, such challenges may sound too enormous to attempt, hence the decision by the victims not to initiate the process of leaving the abuser.

Insufficient Knowledge and Education

Another major issue that creates barriers to help-seeking is a lack of education on the signs of abuse and available resources. Much of the time, victims simply don't identify their experiences as abuse, especially in instances of psychological or emotional abuse where it is not actual physical abuse. Due to this fact, many victims may not perceive their situation as fitting the definition of abuse and, therefore, might not realize that it is actually help-worthy or that they have a right to seek help.

Moreover, many times, the resources and services that exist for the victims of such silent emergencies are not brought out before them. Many may remain ignorant of hotlines, shelters, counseling services, and legal protections that can help them flee from their situations and initiate a recovery process. This lack of knowledge could make the victim feel hopeless and helpless, thereby further reiterating their belief that they have no options or support.

For instance, a person experiencing emotional abuse might begin to understand patterns of manipulation and control as characteristic behaviors, not as abusive actions. If they lack this awareness, they may accept their experience as normal or view themselves as responsible for the problems in the relationship. Similarly, a person whose home has just been invaded is perhaps unaware of which services their community offers to victims of crime, for example, trauma counseling or legal aid, and thus continues to suffer with little to no help.

Educational programs to increase awareness of the signs of abuse and existing resources can be one of the more important means of overcoming this barrier. Such efforts can effectively be carried out through schools, workplaces, and community organizations. Increased awareness through education could help victims overcome part of their shyness and be more confident about seeking the support they need.

Cultural and Religious Barriers

Cultural and religious beliefs can also be big barriers to help-seeking. In some cultures, disclosure of personal or family issues is considered a bad idea; therefore, more emphasis is placed on maintaining family honor and privacy. In order not to shame themselves and their respective families and maintain the dignity of their families, victims may experience a lot of pressure to keep quiet about the abuse.

Religious beliefs can also play the same role in a victim's desire to seek help. Some religious groups are strong in their protection of marriage as an institution and do not believe in divorce or separation; this would even extend to an abusive spouse. Victims may be admonished to pray for their abuser to change his ways or instructed to bear the abuse as part of their cross. Such cultural and religious pressures can make it very difficult for the victims to come out of their abusive situations and seek the necessary help.

For example, a woman being battered by her husband is told to keep the family together at any cost in some cultures. She may be pressured very strongly by her family and leaders of her religion to forgive the abuser and not bring shame to the family. Cultural expectations underpin very strong obstacles that will prevent her from accessing the help needed to empower her to leave the abuse.

Likewise, a victim of a home invasion may not want to report the incident to the police if it is believed that it would shame or dishonor the family or community. He or she may feel that to admit to having been victimized would be to place him or herself in a weak and inept light and result in social ostracism (exclusion) or further victimization.

Overcoming these cultural and religious barriers requires sensitivity and respect. The attitudes of community leaders, religious figures, and cultural organizations can be changed to facilitate the promotion of support for victims. Such leaders, with messages of safety, respect, and compassion, help suppress the stigma attached to asking for help and bring the victims forward.

Insufficient Support Systems

Inadequate formal and informal support systems can substantially hinder a victim's help-seeking efforts. The formal support systems, such as the police, health providers, and social services, may themselves be untrained and ill-equipped to help victims of emergencies in silence adequately. Such searches for services may be met with nonchalant attitudes or even insensitivity and red tape, which further discourage and frustrate the victim.

For example, if a victim of domestic violence were to contact the police or courthouse-based forms of help-seeking, they may be met with skepticism or indifference. They could be told that their situation is not severe enough to elicit intervention, or they may have to endure hours of red tape in an attempt to obtain a restraining order. Negative experiences, such as feelings of distrust, being hassled, and being told that the situation isn't severe enough, deter victims from further help-seeking, culminating in feelings of helplessness and being alone.

These informal systems of support may be insufficient as well. Victims may feel that their loved ones will not be able to understand their situation and hence, therefore, may not be in a position to help them. Friends and family members sometimes contribute to the victim's isolation by downplaying the abuse or by not coming forward with their own experiences of the abuser's behavior. Because such a network of help and support cannot be found, the victim most often feels totally on their own with no one to turn to for assistance in finding their way.

For example, a home invasion victim may turn to their family and be told that they are 'overreacting' or that they 'should have been more careful.' This can create a general lack of empathy and understanding on the part of others, exaggerating in the victim a sense of isolation and helplessness, and perhaps making it much harder to turn to formal support systems.

Formal support systems themselves require training and resources to make their professionals capable of handling these situations with sensitivity and compassion. It implies the training of law enforcement officers for appropriate identification and response to incidents involving domestic abuse, home invasion, and kidnappings, and resourcing healthcare providers for the necessary help in taking care of the victim.

Legal and Bureaucratic Hurdles

Other key challenges to help-seeking come from legal and bureaucratic hurdles. Confronting the legal world can be highly intimidating for victims of silent emergency situations, especially if they are traumatized by their experiences. Getting restraining orders, filing criminal charges, and fighting custody battles for their children all require rather intricate legal processes that take time, money, and emotional stamina.

In so many instances, victims may have absolutely no means of representation or even know about their legal rights. It is the fear of coming face-to-face with the abuser again and the delay associated with the possible lengthy litigation that serves to dissuade victims from seeking help. In addition, red tape, as exemplified by delays in processing applications for social services or difficulties encountered in accessing housing and access to financial services, could all combine to frustrate the entire help-seeking process.

For example, an abused person may need to apply for a restraining order by filing lengthy paperwork, going to several court hearings, and providing voluminous proof of the abuse. Doing all these will exhaust any person, let alone someone who is already suffering from the psychological and emotional consequences of his or her situation. Without legal help, too many victims may give up before they even begin.

For instance, in cases where one has been a victim of a house invasion, the process for filing insurance claims or getting financial aid for repairing damages to his or her house may become very hard to achieve. These bureaucratic hurdles add to the stress and trauma that comes with the event itself, thus making it harder for the victim to overcome these wounds.

These legal and bureaucratic hurdles can only be overcome by making the involved help-seeking processes less complicated and more streamlined. It may include legal aid, advocacy services, and the availability of social services that are easily accessible and responsive to victims' needs.

Psychological Barriers

Fear, denial, and self-blame are some of the major psychological barriers that can drastically affect a victim's ability to seek help. Paralyzing fear of not being believed, of losing custody of the children, or of being homeless may hinder the actions of victims. Another very potent psychological barrier is denial; some victims downplay the fact that things are that bad or that it will get better, the abuse is their fault.

This is a common problem with victims of silent emergency situations: self-blame. One major way this happens is through manipulation on the part of the abuser, who generally convinces the victim that they are to blame for the abuse. Shame and guilt hence get Islamized, making it hard for them to visualize themselves as deserving of help or support— thereby their abusive situations are formed.

For instance, a person who has been abused at home may feel that they somehow caused the abuse to occur or deserve it in some way for having failed to do something right. This sort of self-blaming might be further supported by the abuser through different manipulating actions, all the more putting a victim into a difficult position to get out and ask for help. Another example is that he or she who has been a victim of a home invasion may feel partially guilty due to a lack of better safety measures and thus be reluctant to seek help.

Other psychological barriers include a loss of trust in others, especially when the victim has been double-crossed or manipulated by persons with whom they had put their trust. Due to this distrust, seeking help becomes hard as one might have a fear of experiencing further harm or exploitation.

Such psychological barriers can only be overcome by sensitive, trauma-informed care and support, which recognizes and deals with the very complex emotional and psychic consequences of abuse and other silent emergencies. Counseling and therapy can play a major role in helping victims process their experiences and assist them in building the resilience and confidence to seek help.

Geographic and Logistical Barriers

Other geographic and logistic barriers may isolate a victim from help. For instance, living in a rural or remote area, isolated from access to support services, shelters, or availability of legal aid, creates vulnerability. Access to such facilities is impossible for the victim due to a lack of means of transportation, especially if they do not have a car or access to public transportation.

Some of these logistical hurdles are a little more complicated, such as childcare or other dependents. Many find it hard to find trustworthy childcare, and what is safe to leave them with, in order to go off to appointments, court hearings, or counseling. Keeping one's job or managing the household might further limit the time and energy available to seek help.

For example, in rural areas, a victim may have to drive huge mileages to seek shelter or counseling services. The time and cost of these trips may be too great, especially if the victim is poor. Similarly, childcare while attending court hearings or sessions of counseling may be particularly hard to find for a single parent, making the pursuit of aid quite hardly achievable.

Overcome these geographical and logistical barriers by embracing technological innovations. Mobile applications, online counseling services, and support groups run virtually offer easily accessible and discreet support for the victims, in particular, those dwelling in remote or rural areas. We can make the most of technology in such a way that all victims, no matter where they are, or how distance makes support challenging, receive the same amount of support.

Overcoming Barriers to Help-Seeking

The adoption of a multi-dimensional approach ensures that the various social, cultural, legal, and psychological factors at play are considered when overcoming the barriers to help-seeking in situations of silent emergencies. There is also a need to heighten public awareness creation and education about silent emergency situations and the available facilities. This can reduce the stigma associated with these experiences through public campaigns and encourage victims to come out without their fear of being judged.

In this regard, training and sensitizing professionals like law enforcement officers, medical professionals, and social workers aid in better response to victims and that they get professional support with compassion. Available multifaceted support services of assistance to victims from the hotlines, shelters, legal aid, counseling, and so on do help them find their way through the labyrinthine process.

Informed victims of their rights and the resources available to them are better placed to act. Community-based organizations and advocacy groups can serve as an important means for getting this information out and assisting victims through the process of seeking help. Attention to financial dependence is realized by providing economic support in terms of opportunities that can make the victim financially independent. This may include job training, financial support, and housing arrangements that ensure victims can live safely and have a stable abode.

Changing these cultural and religious barriers will require engagement with the community through dialogue in promoting values of safety, respect, and support for everyone. Another way is to engage religious and cultural leaders through advocacy in protecting the rights of victims to have an effect on changing the mindset.

Most importantly, technological innovations can greatly help surmount geographical and logistical barriers. In particular, mobile applications, online counseling services, and virtual support groups are especially suitable for victims who require discreet support, particularly in remote or rural areas.

The solution to the barriers to seeking help in silent emergency situations needs to be comprehensively worked out through collaboration. Equipped with the knowledge and penetration of the complex social, cultural, legal, psychological, and logistical circumstances that prevent a victim from seeking help, we shall be better placed to begin the support for millions of people affected by domestic abuse, home invasions, kidnappings, and other silent emergencies. The more we know, the more we educate ourselves, and the more easily accessible, compassionate services we provide, the further empowered the victims will feel to seek help and embark on negotiating the road to healing and recovery.

Section 3:

Tech Intervention in Silent Emergency Situations

3.1: Overview of Tech Interventions

Types of Tech Interventions

Technology is key in situations of silent emergencies when the victims cannot call for help in most cases. The situational examples of such silent emergencies are the cases of domestic abuse when a victim has to turn to stealthy ways for help not to alert their abusers. Tech interventions provide innovative solutions to ensure the safety and support of distressed people. These technologies have a wide range, creating several opportunities for the victim to get help without incurring any extra suspicion from the abusive partner. Technology has come of age to provide many tools and resources that have made the process of help-seeking much easier for victims while they remain safe and anonymous.

Applications

Silent emergencies like abuse need quiet yet powerful technological solutions to ensure the safety and support of the victim. Mobile technology's importance is heightened by the fact that it can offer support and give immediate assistance to victims of domestic abuse.

For example, the application Silent Safety helps in that moment of silent emergency, sending messages to the police or family members without any noise. It uses soundless SOS buttons, location-sharing, and real-time updates to offer help in time for safety. The silent alert system of this app may be activated in the presence of abusers by pressing a button on the phone or another wearable device. The ease of use and stealth of this application make it a crucial tool in situations where overt actions might escalate the danger. These types of applications are useful in a multitude of situations where the user cannot speak; some of these situations include domestic abuse and home invasions.

Alongside Silent Safety, multiple mobile apps have been created to help people in such situations. They provide silent notifications, GPS tracking, and alarm messaging to emergency contacts. For instance, bSafe can generate fake calls, send SOS messages, and share the user's location, while Hollie Guard sends automatic alerts and records evidence when activated. These kinds of apps can be engineered to give an assurance of safety so that just in case of anything, help is quickly summoned without necessarily endangering the user.

Panic Buttons

In the cases of silent emergencies, there is an important need to have secret safety measures, such as a panic button, which ensures safety with very quick responses in times of crisis. A panic button silently prevents escalation and offers victims a tactical advantage, which will increase their protection by facilitating rapid responses to their emergencies.

The ADT Panic Button is an excellent example that could be beneficial. These devices are discreetly placed so that one can trigger them without alerting the perpetrator, thereby avoiding harm. The ADT Panic Button can be installed in different places, such as under a desk, inside a closet, or even beside beds. It helps the victim to contact authority inconspicuously without speaking when their lives are in danger. The device offers a single touch to trigger an alarm to the monitoring center or loved ones. Those features allow a home to be safe by responding promptly to emergencies, ensuring maximum safety for those at risk. The ADT Panic Button offers discrete and reliable means through which individuals and families under domestic abuse will be able to use the button without alerting the person abusing them. In the event of a home invasion, it provides a discrete way for residents to raise an alarm with the authorities. It creates instant alarms in house security systems, making the police more equipped to respond and catch the invaders.

A silent alarm system ensures safety for the abused residents, not from the abusers alone but also rescues them from potential confrontations that may cause harm or injuries. Panic buttons are among the exceptionally useful tools for mitigating risk and offering a rapid response in critical situations such as domestic abuse and forced entry into homes. They could prove to be useful in situations that would need someone to get help while having to remain silent.

Wearable Devices

Wearables have reinvented personal safety by taking advanced features and fitting them into everyday wearable gear to make self-defense and safety much easier without raising suspicion. It is in this gear that safety tools are embedded into things people already wear, such as jewelry and fitness bands, to make sure that help is always available.

Wearable devices, like the Apple Watch and invisaWear, have become very important tools for personal safety due to their discrete nature. The Apple Watch contains an SOS feature, where a silent alert and location are sent to emergency contacts; this feature will be quite helpful in cases where silence is required, as in a home invasion or kidnapping. In addition, this watch has an internal GPS that will pinpoint the user's exact location to enable a quick response. The watch is something that could allow people to get help while remaining inconspicuous.

The smart jewelry brand, invisaWear, includes necklaces and bracelets with panic buttons concealed within them, stylishly functional in secretly signaling distress. These jewelry pieces look like standard accessories but contain a hidden button that sends an emergency message. They send information such as location details to the user's selected contacts when clicked. Therefore, it becomes very handy in cases of domestic abuse where the victim is in a situation where they must call out for help without the abuser noticing, such as when they are kidnapped. It models safety features into everyday things, and these wearables will ensure people always have a secretive way of calling for help. These tools allow users to call for help discreetly wherever they are and are capable of saving many lives.

Encrypted Messaging

One of the most important tools in the digital age is encrypted messaging, which offers a secure platform for users to communicate, protect information, and maintain privacy. With growing fears about surveillance, breaches, and protections for personal security, encrypted messaging apps have made a name for themselves. Examples of these apps are Signal and Telegram. These platforms ensure that only the person to whom it was addressed can read messages, providing security protection for delicate conversations and sensitive information. High-tech encryption used by these apps helps people communicate in dangerous situations.

Apps like Signal and Telegram provide secure, silent one-on-one communication where privacy and discretion are important. Signal provides end-to-end encryption, which enables only the recipient to actually read it. Additionally, Signal enables setting silent notifications, furthering a possible victim of domestic abuse's ability to communicate secretly with trusted contacts while the abuser is unaware. This depth of safety is especially important in situations when a victim has to share sensitive information or discreetly work out a plan to remain safe. The app became the go-to choice for people looking to maintain secure communication under threat due to its encryption and privacy safeguards.

Another widely used encrypted messaging app is Telegram, which has a number of features aimed at improving personal safety. Among the popular features of Telegram is self-destructing messages; all sensitive communications are deleted automatically after some stipulated time to prevent the information from being discovered by an abuser or intruder. Another critical feature is an encrypted chat option wherein the messages will remain confidential and cannot be intercepted, which is very important in discreetly sending distress messages or coordinating plans for safety. It ensures secure sharing not only of text messages but also photos, videos, and other media between users to enable completely private communication.

Signal and Telegram, by offering the security of a silent means of communication in times of great need, ensure that a person can feel safe while getting the required help. Such applications give a person peace of mind and a reliable way of maintaining contact with trusted individuals in times of crisis. The users can share their location, describe what's taking place, and get further instructions or reassurance from authorities or loved ones, all through secure messaging, without jeopardizing their safety. The advanced encryption and privacy features within these apps make them very important tools in personal security, enabling users to negotiate perilous situations with far greater levels of confidence and security.

Smart Home Camera Systems

Smart home camera systems have redefined home safety by integrating state-of-the-art technologies that can offer protection and discreet alerting capabilities. Due to growing security threats, systems similar to Ring Alarm and Nest Secure reassure homeowners about comprehensive monitoring and silent notification features. These systems are designed to detect and respond to security breaches without alerting intruders. In some cases, they provide critical time for either occupants to get to safety or to report the crime to appropriate law enforcement. Assuring that homes are kept secure and help can silently be summoned in times of need by leveraging the latest in smart home technology, these systems are very helpful.

Smart home camera systems, such as the Ring Alarm and Nest Secure, allow for good security with silent alerting abilities. Ring Alarm has features that include door and window sensors, motion detection, and cameras capable of silently passing information to the house owner and authorities for action in response to a security breach. Such scenarios would involve home invasion, where time is paramount in helping the victim further hide or flee. A smartphone application allows one to take control of the system, monitor the home environment from anywhere, and get an update on alerts. This feature in the remote control will ensure that the owner stays updated on the threats even when away from home, thus giving a suitable response. The camera on the Ring Alarm can be used to see who is coming near the user's house so that they can respond accordingly to any potential danger. For example, if someone abusing the user were to come to the user's house, they would be able to see that and can call for help to remain safe. The product allows the user to stay secure from potentially threatening people.

The Nest Secure has perfect integration with Google Home, providing complete security and the capability for programming silent alerts to ensure everything is alright in case of any events, such as a door being forced open or a window shattered. Therefore, people can easily manage and view anything from any place. It helps ensure the homeowner is alerted to any potential threats. The Nest Secure integrates security features with smart home applications to ensure a secure environment at home. It allows users to remain secure in their homes due to its many features.

Ring Alarm and Nest Secure improve the safety and security of a home and its occupants. Advanced technologies and integrations make these gadgets so valuable in fending off and responding to potential security threats silently yet effectively.

Biometric Control Systems

Biometric and access control technologies have improved home safety to discrete methods against forced entry. The technologies are supposed to be prerequisites of a modern home: convenient, secure, and able to trigger an alert in silence. With the adoption of biometric technology and smart access control, a house owner can keep their property safe while they respond to threats in silence.

The Samsung SHS-P718 Smart Door Lock exemplifies this advanced approach to home security. Utilizing fingerprint technology, the SHS-P718 can ensure silent access to the home, yet act as a secure access control method, allowing only those authorized to gain entrance. In instances of domestic abuse, this system silently alerts authorities in cases of unauthorized entry attempts into the home, thus improving security without alerting the abuser. This feature adds an extra layer of safety and security to a home in the presence of any threat. That quiet alert in high-risk scenarios is very important for a victim to grab those life-saving seconds to get into a place of safety or launch any other action.

The Samsung SHS-P718 works smoothly with other smart devices, allowing owners to monitor access and control the lock remotely via a smartphone app. This remote functionality for the control means that the homeowner shall be informed and empowered to act in response to the threats, even when he or she is away. Real-time reception of alerts and lock control from anywhere easily contribute to an added layer of convenience and security of management in protecting the home environment. Another way the product can be used is by placing the lock in the house to restrict possible threats from the place where someone is hiding. It would make it harder to enter and buy time, which could be the deciding factor between safety and harm.

Advanced biometric and state-of-the-art access control systems integrated into the security setup of a house guarantee to make any home a safe and secure environment against domestic abuse, home invasion, or even kidnapping threats. With remote control and real-time alert features, a homeowner can ensure protection and take necessary action against impending danger effectively.

Benefits of Tech Intervention

Mobile technology and telehealth services provide support and assistance in real-time to those who are based in remote or underserved areas. Certain applications aid victims of domestic abuse in sending messages to the police or family without having to make any noise. These apps use a variety of methods and features to offer help in time for safety. These applications are hence very vital tools during any clandestine operation where overt action might increase the risk.

Mobile communication platforms facilitate the speedy transmission of information, engage in enlightenment, and provide coordination of responses. Through mobile, an extended crisis is able to communicate effectively, thus keeping the affected population informed and engaged. Cloud-based engagement tools offer human organizations an avenue for the efficient management of partnerships and coordination of efforts; this becomes very crucial for streamlining operations and generally enhancing the efficiency of the responses.

Many devices are discreet, so they provide unobtrusive, personal safety features, like the transmission of silent alerts that include location to emergency contacts. These are very useful in scenarios where silence is key. Some devices are designed to fit seamlessly into everyday life unnoticeably. The majority of the devices are created to resemble ordinary artifacts such as a watch, a bracelet, or some beads and pendants, which are not very likely to be noticed. This subtle appearance comes in handy, especially when one has to avoid suspicion or unwanted attention, such as in hostile surroundings. They make it easier for a person to ensure his safety without blowing his cover or raising an alarm on probable threats.

Sensitive information is highly secured to ensure privacy and safety. Some platforms contain features that ensure that messages are only readable by the recipient to which they are addressed, very useful in cases where messages must be discreet. Besides, secure communication tools are designed to infiltrate into the life of everyday digital interactions. Their subtle appearance particularly comes in handy in situations where one does not want to arouse suspicion or attract attention, like when one is in dangerous neighborhoods or involved in covert operations. A user can be private without giving away anything to harmful people and threats.

Limitations of Tech Intervention

Not everyone has equal access to using technology. For example, in some of the world's most remote and impoverished areas, infrastructure like connectivity and phones is largely absent or limited, thereby limiting the reach of any tech interventions. Moreover, low technological literacy levels are a constraint to effectively using digital tools in growing regions. Capacity-building and training will be required but are resource- and time-intensive operations.

Major privacy risks are related to the collection and storage of sensitive data, especially health-related information. Ensuring the security of that data and the confidentiality of users is important to building and maintaining the trust of affected communities. Heavier reliance on technology opens systems to cyber threats such as hacking, breaches, and ransomware attacks. Proper cybersecurity measures will be required to ensure the integrity of tech interventions.

Execution and maintenance of technological solutions are very resource-intensive, as they consume funding, technical expertise, and further maintenance support. Such interventions are hard to sustain in resource-poor environments. There are risks brought by dependence on technology, such as technical failures that can contribute to the crisis through malfunctioning of the systems, software bugs, and hardware problems that might disrupt services.

3.2: Communication and Support Platforms

Online Support Groups

Online support provides a much-needed platform for those suffering from cases of domestic abuse. The platforms provide anonymity that helps the victims to share their experiences and get advice on how to deal with the problem while thereof avoiding retaliation from their abusers. The anonymity of the online support groups is most important as it gives victims the ability to discuss their situations openly and freely and to get the help they need without putting themselves in further danger. For instance, from online forums, like Reddit's r/domesticviolence, to focused websites, like DailyStrength, individuals can connect with others who understand their struggles in a moderated, confidential environment. These communities can offer emotional support, a means of sharing some of the important resources, legal advice, and contact information of the local shelters or support services, all of which are ready to help someone 24/7.

Online support groups are available 24/7 so they can offer help whenever it is needed, hence being able to give comfort and assistance immediately in the worst of times. In contrast to the traditional support groups, which hold meetings at specific times, these online platforms remain open all day and night for the victims to reach for support whenever they intend to. Apart from that, the dissemination of educational materials and self-help resources arms the victim with the knowledge to sail safely through their situation. Isolation won't trouble those who feel very alone in their struggles because groups can offer a sense of community and solidarity. A support system never out of reach may be important to people who are really lost.

Crisis Text Lines and Chatbots

Crisis text lines and chatbots are tools that give silent and immediate support to people in distress, especially to those who cannot make a call without putting their safety in jeopardy. The services offered are discreet and confidential in nature, where victims can obtain help and advice in real-time. For example, Crisis Text Line allows individuals to send an anonymous message to trainers who return responses to such requests 24/7. This service helps victims with absolutely essential access to help at all times of the day or any time of distress. Similarly, AI-powered chatbots like Woebot offer mental health support through text-based interactions that provide ways to cope and find help in privacy and discretion.

Confidentiality and discretion offered by crisis text lines and chatbots are crucial for someone in an abusive situation, where any overt action may escalate the danger. These very tools can be leveraged by victims to communicate silently, securely, and in such a manner that they will not set off alert abusive partners. These platforms often provide the user with huge amounts of valuable information on safety planning and emergency resources that users may draw upon in taking proactive steps for protection. The anonymity and immediate availability of such services make these supports valuable to victims.

Telehealth Services for Therapy and Counseling

Domestic abuse victims can get professional help without having to step out of their homes, which could considerably benefit from telehealth services in terms of accessibility to therapy and counseling. These services will, therefore, give the user access to licensed therapists through video calls, phone calls, or even messaging. This is consequently a convenient way of getting mental health support. Geographical barriers have been eliminated as a hindrance to services with the rise of platforms such as BetterHelp and Talkspace. This is particularly important for people who reside in remote or unserved areas and would otherwise not have had access to traditional in-person therapy services. These services could provide much-needed help to people that experienced traumatic situations and are in need of help to move on from them.

It gives domestic abuse victims privacy and safety through telehealth services because a victim can attend as many therapy sessions as they need to from any safe location without fear of being discovered by the abusers. In doing so, it gives them the emotional support and guidance they need to navigate their situation safely and effectively. It can also be beneficial after they escape the situation since it would have been a difficult experience. Another feature of the majority of telehealth services is the inclusion of secure messaging and anonymous chat options, which help user security and privacy. It is very important to provide a safe and accessible way for people in silent emergencies to get professional mental health support. Telehealth helps people to develop some resilience and coping strategies towards their situations.

Apps for Domestic Abuse Education

Education always takes a very empowering approach to fighting domestic abuse, and specialized apps and websites are involved in this cause by delivering substantive information and resources to victims and society as a whole. Aspire News and Bright Sky are educational apps that provide wide knowledge about the identification of abuse, legal rights, and access to local support services. Hidden features in these apps, disguised interfaces, and emergency alert systems all help ensure the safety of users. By inconspicuously accessing basic information that empowers a victim to seek help and protection measures without raising suspicion, these apps become key to protection.

In addition, there are informative websites of the National Domestic Violence Hotline and Women's Aid that present long chains of resources, including guides on safety planning and legal advice, and contact details of support services. These centers also spread awareness about domestic abuse through such websites and encourage the victims to come out and seek help. The websites provide information regarding the identification of the problem and how early intervention is very necessary. These educational materials are therefore very important in diffusing information and skills to the victim and to the general public to enable them to assist the abused.

Social Media Campaigns and Stories

Social media has thus become a very strong means of raising awareness about domestic abuse and providing victims with a platform to come out and speak. Hashtag campaigns like #MeToo and #WhyIStayed have brought the issue of domestic abuse to the very frontline globally, acting as a forum from which victims could share their stories to find others who have gone through similar experiences. Like this, such campaigns have helped reduce the stigma placed on domestic abuse, encouraging victims to seek help.

Social media groups and pages established for domestic abuse survivors allow members to share their experiences, and find support, and even resources. For example, Facebook groups can be an area where, openly, the victims can discuss with other people who appreciate their plight and who will be very supportive and encouraging. In the same breath, public figures are known to bring issues to light by using their platforms to support those affected by domestic violence, sharing resources, and spreading awareness. This not only increases their visibility but serves to further amplify the message as many more witnesses come into action against domestic abuse. Social media. campaigns and stories are important for creating a supportive community.

Section 4:

Implementation and Future Directions

4.1: Challenges in Implementing Tech Solutions

Privacy and Security concerns

As technology continues integrating into everyday life, issues threatening safety have surfaced. These problems occur through all forms of technology, varying in complexity. Companies discovered it useful to use consumer data for targeted advertising rather than only storing the data needed for their functions. Technology users are at constant risk of having their privacy violated, and only 5% of consumers possess no major concerns over how organizations use their data (MAGNA/Ketch).

It's important to be able to distinguish between privacy and security to determine a specific concern. Privacy is the right to control your personal information. Security, on the other hand, refers to the protection of personal information. As technology advances, privacy is a vital issue for consumer protection. Data that is stored by businesses and apps are at risk of being stolen through cyberattacks. Cybersecurity is the form of internet security that attempts to fight against cyberattacks, aiming to keep private information safe.

Privacy issues are particularly prevalent in computer science. These problems arise primarily through unauthorized data collection, advertising, and data and surveillance breaches. Personal customer information is included in 44% of data breaches, in which information such as a customer's name, email, and password is leaked (IBM). All online actions leave a trace of data that can be gathered and eventually leaked. Some issues formed around internet 'cookies', which are data files stored on your computer that have the potential to track internet activity.

Security issues also cause trouble to cybersecurity, which is the practice of protecting computer systems, networks, and data from attacks. There are numerous cyber threats that have the ability to cause significant damage if not dealt with properly. Cybercrimes such as identity theft, phishing, and hacking aim to obtain and gain access to sensitive information and data. Ransomware, a kind of malicious software, has recently turned into a popular form of cyberattack. Ransomware is made to block access to a victim's computer files or system until a ransom is paid to the attacker, and the average ransom demand in 2021 was 5.3 million USD (ISACA).

Fortunately, there are ways that consumers can protect their data. It's highly recommended that users backup their data on a regular basis so that the risk of losing their data is minimized. One of the simplest ways to keep your data secure is to use strong unique passwords that are difficult to guess and multi-factor authentication if available. You should also learn to detect suspicious emails as phishing emails are starting to become more detailed and common. Anti-virus software is available to protect your device against malware to ensure that devices are secure at all times. When using public Wi-Fi you can use a secure Virtual Private Network(VPN) for a secure connection with fewer risks of revealing personal data. Taking these practices into account will ensure that you and your personal information are less likely to be leaked or stolen.

While all the information previously mentioned targeted concerns regarding the internet and devices, there are other forms of technology that aren't immune to unwanted access. Security cameras can put your data at risk, as they can be hacked in multiple ways. Phishing can also be used for hackers to gain access to the camera feed, as well as bugs and glitches in your camera. A couple of the security issues that cause cybersecurity threats can also occur to security cameras. Having your security camera hacked can jeopardize the safety of your entire security system. It can also put the safety of your entire household at risk due to the amount of information that can be leaked when cameras are hacked.

Luckily, there are ways to combat the troubles associated with security cameras. The primary method is to purchase cameras from companies with high-quality security practices and powerful reputations. Companies such as Arlo, Ring, Nest, and Blink are known to have the best home security cameras. There are many guides available to help you choose the right camera for you and your safety. Make sure to constantly update your camera's firmware to prevent security holes that can make your computer vulnerable to hacking. Not all cameras update automatically, so you may have to do it manually.

It's important to take note of the signs that can let you know if your security camera has been hacked. Unknown account information or new logins can reveal unwanted access or that your camera has been hacked. To prevent a scenario like this, you should create a strong password that can be generated with a password manager. You should also enable two-factor authentication if possible so that even if your password is guessed by someone, they still won't be able to gain access to your account. If your camera has speakers that can turn on, hearing strange noises coming from the camera can be a sign of hacking. Unusual movements of your camera, such as rotation or pivoting on its own, can mean that it was accessed by a stranger. To find out more, you can check the camera's access and login history.

Technology is growing at a rapid rate, and along with it comes the development and sophistication of attacks that threaten devices. It's necessary to be aware of the risks that technology is vulnerable to and the methods that can be used to keep yourself and your data safe.

Accessibility and user-friendliness

In regards to technology, accessibility is when technology can be used by an audience with a large range of abilities and disabilities. User-friendliness is the idea that the technology is engaging and easy to use for all users. When it comes to the relationship between the two, accessibility can be used to help with the extent to which user-friendliness applies to all users. Technology with more accessibility is more likely to be user-friendly.

Accessible technology includes aspects of universal design in which users are able to use the technology in the way that works best for them. Accessible technology can be used with or without the help of assistive technology. Technology without the help of assistive technology can be deemed as directly accessible. On the other hand, technology without the aid of assistive technology is consistent with standard assistive technology. Accessible technology can be used by a wide range of audiences, like how elevators are accessible to both wheelchair users and non-wheelchair users. Accessible technology can be used by users with impairments and disabilities, such as audio, visual, and speech impairments.

There are many kinds of accessible devices and products that are designed in a way that can be used by a broad range of individuals. Websites that are accessible are made so all users can navigate and interact with the site. Accessible websites offer text equivalents for all non-text elements, including audio, video, graphics, animation, and image maps. Accessible multimedia products offer more than one way to interact with and respond to the device. They include text captions and audio descriptions for visual content. Copy machines that are accessible use voice recognition, keypads, or touch screens. They are easily adjustable and are put within reach of all users. Accessible software applications usually have specific features. They don't use just color to spread information and provide user guides in different formats, like braille or electronic text.

User-friendly technology is exactly what it sounds like. It is a technique that aims to provide a satisfying experience to all users. User-friendly technology is efficient and easy to use, allowing users to accomplish their tasks with minimal effort. It prioritizes the user, letting a wide range of users be able to understand and enjoy the technology without facing any challenges.

When it comes to the design and specifics of the technology, user-friendliness involves multiple principles aimed at creating interfaces that are efficient, and pleasant to use while prioritizing usability. Users should be able to interact with the technology without needing a great deal of prior knowledge. The application should have clarity so that users can understand the technology. The clarity of text is specifically important. Many users have visual impairments, so the text should be clear and concise. The aesthetics and design of the interface should be consistent so that it can provide familiarity and be visually appealing to the user's eye. User-friendly technology gives the user the necessary feedback to navigate through any changes or problems. The technology should be flexible enough so users can make necessary adjustments to their preferences. The design should also be responsive, meaning that it can adjust based on the device and can be used on many platforms. Although user-friendliness is meant to be simple for the user, it is complex in design and incorporates multiple elements and techniques.

Connecting back to the definition of user-friendliness itself, user-friendly technology should be accessible, which is where accessibility and user-friendliness meet to create the best user experience. When accessibility and user-friendliness combine, they create a form of technology that is far more advanced and satisfactory than others. Unique functionality and features are created that contribute largely to inclusivity and support of users. For example, take websites. Websites are created to provide information and solutions. If many people can use the website, an inclusive web design is created. When websites are created with inclusive web design regulations, a high number of users are ensured to be able to access the website. A wide audience paves the way for inclusivity, leading to more user interaction and as a result user-friendliness. Accessibility is used as the foundation for user-friendliness. The technology aims to provide a positive experience for users based on the range of users that is determined by the accessibility of the technology.

While they are different concepts, accessibility and user-friendliness work best together. It's difficult to have one without the other, and together they provide a seamless and inclusive experience. Accessibility guarantees that users with disabilities can use and access a website or devices, while user-friendliness is the idea of making the application appeal to all audiences and provide satisfaction to all users. When the two are integrated, the result is a technology that enhances a positive user experience that can be accessed by a broad audience. Increased efficiency and engagement are produced as a result. When accessibility and user-friendliness are prioritized, an environment is made where all users are valued and can effortlessly interact with the technology.

Resource allocation

Resource allocation is the idea of distributing and managing resources to support organization and planning. Its role is vital in technology as it helps to determine how materials are utilized to meet technological goals.

Companies use project management software to implement resource allocation. Since it is difficult to monitor and plan out multiple projects at the same time, PM software is used to automate the process. When using the software, a company can track people and resources related to multiple projects simultaneously. The software saves a great deal of time and effort for companies, allowing them to effectively manage their tasks while having the time to do other things.

Although technology is worth investing in, it can be expensive when it comes to money. Thus, resource allocation is used for budgeting and spending the money efficiently. By allocating financial resources, companies are utilizing technology beneficial to their development. When money is allocated effectively it can be properly funded for technology initiatives.

While resource allocation can be used for technology, technology can also be utilized for resource allocation. Investing in technologies like the PM software mentioned above can significantly boost productivity. AI, blockchain, and IoT are prime examples of the technology that can help companies allocate their resources.

Using resource allocation in relation to technology ensures that resources are available at the right time and are used in a beneficial way. As a result, innovation is fostered while the productivity of a company is maximized.

Funding and product management

As stated previously, technology can be quite expensive. Resource allocation is one of the more helpful methods that can be used to afford technology, but a company still must have proper funding in order to purchase new technologies while also having to buy other equipment at the same time for them to survive. Technologies can be funded through various means, including but not limited to cash grants and donations.

Funding allows for more development towards research and development(R&D). Research and development lets companies develop prototypes and explore new ideas. However, without adequate funding, it would be difficult to progress. Activities would be limited and the technological progress would be slowed as a result. Product development is also affected by funding. A large amount of money is required to develop new products, especially technology products. Investments must be made in the development and design of the product, as well as the testing and overall production of it. These processes can only be achieved with thorough funding and may require even more to produce the desired results.

A certain set of individuals are required to build and use these technologies. However, it is expensive to hire and attract talented workers in the top engineering and science fields. Companies will want to hire the right audience by offering salaries and benefits that are both competitive and rewarding. Adequate funding would allow for a skilled workforce that can both create and put technology to use. Even after workers are hired, though, resources and processes must be used to create more technology. It requires even more money to build and maintain products. With funding, the proper amount of money would be put to use to ensure these components are locked in place.

After creating a product, it must be advertised to gain popularity and sales. Marketing and sales require more effort and money. Funding would support these efforts, which include advertising, campaigns, and training for sales teams. All of these activities would ensure promotional success for the technology product and can be accomplished through funding.

Products must also adhere to regulatory requirements, which can be significantly costly especially when it comes to the finance and healthcare industries. Funding lets these companies meet the requirements without having to worry about the product's safety or compromise the product's quality.

Products can get stolen or hacked, so measures must be taken to protect the safety of technology products. It's essential to invest in cybersecurity and risk management to protect technological assets and the data they possess. Funding would allow for these security measures to be implemented effectively without any further risk.

Funding can also facilitate collaborations and partnerships with other corporations to gain support and assistance for a product or technology. These collaborations will help improve the technological advancements of a company's product and help it grow. Partnerships can be done with universities, research institutions, and other organizations. When money is needed for these partnerships, funding will help in supplying the needed resources.

Environmental sustainability practices have become increasingly popular, and it would be a smart idea for companies to implement them in their technology products. However, it is expensive to create technology that is environmentally sustainable due to all the steps needed to create it. With adequate funding, technology can be implemented with sustainable manufacturing processes and renewable energy systems that will allow companies to follow green technology initiatives.

Once a product starts to get successful and gain popularity, technology companies may want to expand internationally. Funding is especially important to explore new markets and regulations and may even have to change the product to fit the local needs of other countries.

In summary, funding is crucial for the innovation of technology. Every stage in the production and development of a product can only be done with proper funding, from research to expansion. Funding essentially influences a company's ability to innovate technology and produce successful products.

4.2: Best Practices for Tech Development

Involving survivors in the design process

When technology is made to help people, one of the best methods in designing the product is to include the intended audience of the product in the process. Specifically when it comes to trauma, it would be difficult to create a product made to help with a survivor's trauma without getting to know the survivor. Implementing users in the design process would be beneficial because the design can be tailored specifically to their needs and adjusted to their comfort.

It's critical to involve survivors in the design process so that the product can respond to them effectively. Designers usually conduct interviews with survivors to understand their situation. There is information about trauma survivors that can only be obtained through the victims as they are the ones who experienced it firsthand. Their story and feelings are crucial to the technology.

User-centered design(UCD) is an iterative process in which designers focus exclusively on the user's experience. An iterative process is a process in which teams repeatedly build, test, and revise a product until they are satisfied with the result. In UCD, designers combine investigative and generative methods to create an understanding of the user. Design teams in UCD implement the users throughout the entire design process. Using numerous techniques regarding research and design to connect to the user, they create a product that is highly accessible to them.

Usually, every iteration of UCD has four phases. In the first phase, designers try to determine the setting and context in which users will use their application. In the second phase, the requirements of the user are identified and decided. The third is the design phase where the team generates solutions. In the fourth and final phase, the team assesses the results of an evaluation against the requirements of a user to see how well it performs and matches the user's needs. After all phases are complete, one iteration is finished and the team continues to make iterations until they get the desired results.

Unlike some other design processes, UCD prioritizes the users and creates their entire project around them. The developer of User-centered design, Don Norman, argued that a good design should be centered around the needs of the user rather than the desires of the designer. The design team's goal is to address the entire experience of the survivors. In order to capture their experience, the help of a variety of individuals is needed. Apart from the users themselves, professionals from various fields are needed to carry out the project. Engineers, psychologists, stakeholders, and other experts are also usually involved in the execution of a product. These experts would be able to do the work that designers simply cannot.

It requires a lot of time and effort to collect user data and put it to use, but UCD is generally considered to be worth it in the end. Due to close interaction with the users, the product tends to be more likely to meet users' expectations, which leads to increased sales. Because designers are constantly in contact with survivors, a connection is made between them which results in the creation of an honorable design. Designers create the product for a specific situation and user, so the risk of human error is reduced which makes the product safer.

The way that content is understood by an audience is drastically changed when traumatic events come into play. Anxiety, stress, and trauma change the way that individuals think and make decisions. During high-stress situations, the brain triggers a 'fight or flight' response that focuses solely on survival. Stress has a large impact on how we consume media and content, which is why designers must be careful when designing products that involve survivors' trauma. Stress can cause information to be complex to comprehend which will change a user's experience, and designers must alter their product to react to the user accordingly.

It's important to consider the feelings of the user and let them express their own opinions. When making Scotland's Redress Scheme, which was created to provide compensation for abuse survivors, survivors were asked to complete a sentence that described their experience as an abuse victim. At the time the idea seemed like a quick and simple way to gain information on the potential users of the scheme, but the plan quickly backfired. The survivors despised the idea, saying that they wanted the choice to express as much information as they wanted to and that one simple sentence wasn't enough for them. Survivors want a choice, they want to be respected and heard, which the design team should take into consideration when creating a product that is designed for them.

Trauma-informed care is an approach to care knowledge to gain a complete understanding of a patient's situation. By understanding a survivor's past and present, effective health care can be better offered to them. When it comes to producing a technology that appeals to the same patients, this approach can also be taken.

Five principles must be followed for trauma-informed practice; safety, trust, choice, empowerment, and collaboration. These principles are close-knit and should remain balanced when working with survivors who have experienced trauma. Users should feel comfortable and safe when talking about their experiences, which can be done with the help of these principles. By incorporating these trauma-informed principles to learn more about users, a more welcoming environment is created and the inclusivity can cause survivors to be more open about their trauma which reveals more information that the design team can benefit from greatly.

Designing technology based on the users rather than the designers paves the way for a user-friendly product free from the selfish desires of the designer. The product would have a clear goal and would also be best to achieve that goal because the survivors whom the device was made for contributed to the project. Learning about trauma and using trauma-informed principles for the design will help the team figure out how to reduce stress for their users when using their technology. As TPXimpact says, do research with people, not with people.

Continuous feedback and improvement

Continuous feedback is the idea of sharing feedback at work regularly, typically through a series of conversations. This form of feedback includes any sort of constructive remark or discussion between employees and managers, or between peers.

Unlike providing regular feedback, continuous feedback happens regularly and repeats. Feedback could just be a simple compliment given to an employee by their boss, one that provided a limited amount of comfort and produced no long-term results. However, a small comment of praise could leave the employee craving for more approval, and feeling disheartened after receiving no more. Instead, continuous feedback exists to provide the employee with the approval they desire every so often, mixed with opinions and criticism to elevate their progress. Check-ins don't have much of an effect if they don't happen regularly.

This form of feedback is typically used to address the progress of quality and productivity improvement, so it contains more than just praise. A variety of topics and opinions can be discussed in these conversations, and should not only be focused on satisfaction but improvement too. Difficult topics like criticism shouldn't be avoided because check-ins are supposed to document growth which won't occur easily without some brutal honesty. Everyone benefits from these conversations, as managers can see progress and form better relationships with their employees while employees receive feedback constantly rather than having to wait for the day when their manager would notice them. Trust can be built between individuals and a better work environment can be built with continuous feedback.

Continuous feedback doesn't just have to be one-on-one, it can be used within an entire organization. However, when a whole workforce is involved, it is better to use a continuous feedback loop. A continuous feedback loop is a practice where feedback starts with the employees. Employees provide comments to the leaders of their organization. Their feedback is collected via various methods such as emails or surveys. Leaders and managers then receive and examine the feedback to improve their companies. This method provides satisfaction to the employees because they know that their problems are seen and acknowledged. Knowing that their feedback is considered, employees continue to send such comments to leadership. Thus, a loop is created within the organization and desirable results are achieved.

Continuous feedback is a powerful tool that drives improvement within an organization. It plays a vital role in enhancing a company's performance and fosters growth in multiple areas. It gives support to all workers and lets organizations reach their full potential.

Ensuring accessibility and inclusivity

In regards to technology, accessibility, and inclusivity work hand in hand to create a welcoming product available to a diverse audience. For technology to be inclusive, it must first be accessible.

When technology is accessible, it can be used by a wide range of individuals, including those with disabilities. Since the product appeals to a larger number of people, the product is likely to have a greater number of sales due to the accessibility range. The technology will have the potential to grow quickly in popularity and obtain a high number of consumers with varying backgrounds.

Accessible technology can boost communication between individuals, especially when it is digital. There are many online platforms where consumers can voice their opinions and start discussions with other consumers. When a platform is accessible, individuals from different backgrounds and experiences can connect and feel welcome. For example, video conferencing software allows remote users to be able to participate in meetings. This way colleagues can communicate with one another without having to worry about their differences getting in the way of their contact. Speech recognition software allows people with physical or visual impairments to talk freely the same way as users without disabilities.

Employees should all be able to have equal access to their technology. By ensuring that technology is inclusive, people with disabilities and impairments will be able to access the product. Since these people are able to use the technology, it becomes accessible along with it being inclusive too. Using technology from the broadest range of scenarios is made possible with inclusive design principles that create accessible technologies. Together, inclusivity and accessibility in technology are essential for designing products that can be used by everyone regardless of their abilities and backgrounds.

Inclusivity in technology starts by having a diverse team that creates the product. Having people from various backgrounds create the product will ensure that the result is more likely to reach a broad range of audience. Diverse groups can better fit technology to meet the needs of all potential users. The product can be tailored to fit various needs like color and text adaptability and voice settings. Also, having a diverse group will help reduce bias within the product due to there being a range of unique and contrasting opinions within the team.

Adapting technology to different languages and cultures will be beneficial when you want to expand the product internationally for it to be used by consumers all over the world. Using diversity in the product will give it more representation.

Overall, technology must be inclusive and accessible for it to be beneficial to any and all users. Integrating these into the design and development of a product will boost its audience and acceptance. Inclusivity and accessibility will let technology companies ensure that their products have the ability to serve a large, diverse audience and can promote a more welcoming world digitally.

4.3: The Future of AI

Emerging tech and global implementation

With the discovery of Artificial Intelligence, another layer of production and assistance was added to our daily lives. Improvements in the AI field continue to mold our future in every aspect of life. AI has turned into the primary driver of growing technologies, like robotics and generative AI.

When it comes to understanding AI, it's important to note that there are different types of AI and that there will be more to emerge soon. The first kinds of AI applications were built on traditional machine learning models. Since then, AI has evolved at a steady rate and developed into other versions. More complex AI models are geared to perform human-like tasks without the need for a human brain. While there are many differing types of AI, it can mainly be broken down into two categories which are AI capabilities and AI functionalities.

There are three kinds of AI capabilities. The first is Narrow AI, also known as Weak AI. This is the only form of AI that exists currently. Narrow AI can only perform a specific task, but can usually do so much faster than the human mind can. It can only focus on its assigned task and cannot perform outside of it. Examples of Narrow AI today include voice assistants, chatbots, and self-driving car systems.

The next AI capability is General AI, also referred to as Strong AI. General AI is only theoretical and hasn't been achieved yet. AGI has the ability to use previous skills to accomplish new tasks. This form of AI can understand and apply knowledge across a variety of fields. It is the most similar to human intelligence, as it is meant to be able to perform any task that humans intellectually can. Although it doesn't exist in reality, a fictional example of Strong AI would be Big Hero 6.

The final of the three AI capabilities is Super AI. This form of AI is highly theoretical and subject to debate. Super AI is usually referred to as artificial superintelligence, as it has capabilities so strong that it passes human intelligence. Super AI would make decisions and possess thoughts like no other human can. Super AI is meant to have abilities that are beyond human understanding, having unique desires and emotions.

When it comes to AI functionalities, there are four types. Reactive Machine AI is a type of AI system that has no memory and is only designed to perform a certain task. They only work with data that is currently available in the present. They reach inputs based on outputs that are previously designed and cannot learn from the past. An example of Reactive Machine AI is IBM Deep Blue, which is IBM's chess-playing computer.

Limited Memory is another AI functionality. Unlike Reactive Machine AI this form of AI can recall events from the past. They use data from both the present and past to react to situations. However, they have a limited memory of previous interactions.

The third AI functionality is Theory of mind AI. Theory of Mind AI is a concept that isn't yet developed and doesn't fully exist yet, but it's currently in progress. This AI is advanced and can react to and understand human emotions and beliefs. This AI can interact with humans by responding to their actions. AI researchers are currently trying to develop a Theory of Mind AI, hoping that it can have the ability to analyze data such as images and voices.

The final AI functionality is also currently nonexistent and is entirely hypothetical. Self-aware AI would possess traits of Super AI. Self-aware AI would have its own set of beliefs and emotions while also being able to understand and react to human traits. This AI would have its own conscience and self-awareness, it would be aware of its own existence.

Every type of AI has its own unique strengths and limitations. Artificial Intelligence is a vast and diverse field, filled with programs and machines that will only continue to blow minds. AI is still in development, and high expectations are set out for its future.

Coauthors' Notes

Kenneth Lin

Hey everyone, it's your coauthor Kenneth, and I am here to deliver a background of these fictional stories and of myself in Section 1. So most importantly to note is that Ceaseless– the fictional story told in Section 1.1 is based on multiple real stories submitted by users online to forums, huge organizations, and different websites around the internet. This fictional story uses elements of uncertainty to encapsulate the reader within this universe completely different from theirs. As for myself, I am a student interning at Silent Safety the summer of 2024-2025, and I hope to bring a fresh perspective to the table of different interns as an aspiring STEM student. This unique preference allows me to apply a different perspective in debates, organizing, and more. Although my story will never be as courageous or tumultuous as many of these compiled stories are, I will always try my best to deliver to a greater audience.

Vaibhav Kolli

I'm Vaibhav, coauthor of "Behind Closed Doors". Born and raised in the United States, I grew an interest for video games, sports - such as basketball and football - and spending time with friends and family. My drive in helping to write this book is my passion to spread knowledge and provide precautions/steps to take for those who find themselves in silent safety emergencies. Throughout this book, my main work was covering the types of silent safety emergencies and our society encounters on a day-to-day basis. From domestic abuse to home invasions, I established the basic statistics and information for people to acknowledge the frequency and reality of such situations.

Vikranth Kolluru

I'm Vikranth, one of the coauthors of this book. I moved to the United States when I was a child. I spend most of my time with friends and family. I have an interest in playing video games and listening to music. When I get some free time, I also enjoy playing basketball with my friends. My work for this book consisted of finding information about the types of technologies that can be used in silent emergencies and examples of such technologies as seen in Section 2. I worked on explaining how they can be used, as well as the benefits and limits of the technology. The reason I worked on this book is to help people learn information about how they could be prepared for silent emergencies, which could save lives. I am passionate about helping other people in any way I can and technology. This book gave me the opportunity to make an impact on 2 topics I am passionate about.

Sahana Pulavarthy

Hello, I'm Sahana, one of the coauthors of this book. I live in Texas, which is where I grew up and lived my entire life. I love to read. It's what I spend most of my time doing. However, when my nose isn't deep in a book, you can find me spending time with my friends and family. I also particularly enjoy music and love to try new things. I wrote section four of this book, which consists of the utilization and planning of technological devices, as well as where technology could be heading someday. The section starts out by explaining the various aspects of technology, and the next chapter discusses the techniques and methods that are used to maximize the creation and growth of technology products. Section 4 ends with a short chapter about Artificial Intelligence and how it is expected to turn out in the future. Technology has always particularly caught my interest, which is why I helped write this book and enjoyed doing so.